HOW TO MAKE

MONEY

FROM
COOKING AND
BAKING

RITA STOREY

FRANKLIN WATTS

LONDON • SYDNEY

Franklin Watts
First published in Great Britain in 2017 by
The Watts Publishing Group

Credits
Series editor: Sarah Peutrill
Editor: Sarah Ridley
Packaged by Storeybooks
Designer: Rocket Design (East Anglia) Ltd
Cover design: Peter Scoulding

ISBN 978 1 4451 5280 6

Printed in China

MIX
Paper from
responsible sources
FSC
www.fsc.org
FSC® C104740

Picture acknowledgements
The publisher would like to thank the following for permission to reproduce their photos and pictures: **Cover and title page:** Shutterstock/Perfect Vectors, Daniel Cozma, Vladvm, SelenaMay; Shutterstock/Alkestida 11 (middle top); Shutterstock/bikeriderlondon 5 (bottom); Shutterstock/Boris Bushmin 9; Shutterstock/s-bukley 29 (bottom); Shutterstock/Paola Canzonetta 13 (bottom right); Shutterstock/Rose Carson 20, 27; Shutterstock/daseaford 25 (bottom); Shutterstock/VDex 2, 14 (top); Shutterstock/Doremi 16 (bottom); Shutterstock/ducu59us 12 (middle); Shutterstock/filborg 13 (bottom left), 21, 22 (middle); Shutterstock/frikota 19 (bottom); Shutterstock/JFunk 3 (top), 22 (top), 24 (top); Shutterstock/gourmetphotography 22 (bottom middle); Shutterstock/Alex Gukalov 10 (top); Shutterstock/Monkey Business Images 6 (top), 24 (bottom); Shutterstock/Neizu 3 (bottom right), 10 (bottom), 13 (top left), 18 (top right); Shutterstock/pandora64 26 (middle); Shutterstock/Portare fortuna 17; Shutterstock/Pretty Vectors 11 (bottom), 16 (top); Shutterstock/RedKoala 3 (bottom left); Shutterstock/Viktorija Reuta 18 (top left); Shutterstock/SpeedKingz 19 (top); Shutterstock/subarashii21 5 (top), 6 (bottom), 13 (top right), 14 (bottom), 18 (bottom), 22 (bottom left and right), 26 (bottom), 28, 29 (top); Shutterstock/Tribalium 23; Shutterstock/vector-calculator 11 (top/middle); Shutterstock/vetrovamaria 4 (left); Shutterstock/Vipavienkoff 4 (right).
Every attempt has been made to clear copyright. Should there be any inadvertent omission please apply to the publisher for rectification.

Franklin Watts
an imprint of
Hachette Children's Group
The Watts Publishing Group
Carmelite House
50 Victoria Embankment
London EC4Y 0DZ

An Hachette UK Company
www.hachette.co.uk

www.franklinwatts.co.uk

... is in the food they eat. The consequences of eating the wrong foods can be serious. So label all food products with a list of the ingredients they contain. If you are handling food you will need to comply with food safety and food hygiene regulations. These vary from country to country so be sure to look up what you need to do to make your food products comply.

If you create a very profitable business you will need to pay tax on the money you earn. It is important to keep records of all your sales as well as the receipts for the things you buy to run the business. Tax laws vary from country to country. If your business begins to make money, find out about your business responsibilities.

CONTENTS

WHY START A BUSINESS?

Have you ever dreamed of owning your own cooking or baking business? People who own businesses are called entrepreneurs. They set up their own businesses rather than working for other people. This is called being self-employed. Successful entrepreneurs have the energy and determination to make things happen.

What is a business?

Some businesses make things (goods) that we buy in the shops or online. The cakes and bread in supermarkets and shops are goods.

GOODS

SERVICES

Other businesses provide services. Tea shops and restaurants provide a place where people can be served drinks and food.

The reason for running a business is usually to make money (profit). Some businesses such as charity shops are set up so that the profits help a charity.

Advantages and disadvantages of running your own business

Advantages and rewards

✓ If a business is a success, the reward is the money you make (profit) and the satisfaction that your idea worked.

✓ You are your own boss and no-one tells you what to do.

Disadvantages and risks

✗ If a business fails, the entrepreneur is responsible for any losses.

✗ You have to make all the decisions. The responsibility for the success or failure of the company is yours.

✗ You have to work very hard.

Size of business

A PARTNERSHIP
Two or more people owning a business jointly.

A SOLE TRADER
One person owning a business.

A COMPANY
When a business has shareholders – people who own shares in the business and share the profit.

To start a business you need:

✓ A strong business idea. This is the most important thing. All the hard work you put in could be wasted if the business idea is not strong.

✓ Goods or services to sell, or the equipment and expertise to provide a service.

✓ Money to pay for all the things you need to get the business started. These are called start-up costs. See pages 16–17 for more information.

✓ Customers or consumers: people who will buy the product or service. For your business to make money there must be enough people to buy the products at the price you are charging.

✓ A lot of energy and enthusiasm.

Pages 7, 21, 22 and 24 have fictitious examples of four different types of business, with an explanation of how to start each of them up in order to make a profit.

FINDING A BUSINESS IDEA

Business ideas come from all sorts of places. You might have invented a completely new product, or you may have realised that a group of people need something – and have created a product or service to meet that need. This is called finding a gap in the market. Identifying a gap in the market gives you a perfect business opportunity.

Brainstorming

How to identify a gap in the market

Talk to people to see if there is a new product or service they would like.

If you are working in partnership with others you can brainstorm ideas. This means writing down any business ideas that you can think of, however strange they might be, and discussing each one.

Ideas do not have to be completely new. Sometimes there is room for another business supplying a slightly different version of an existing product or service.

Write down activities you enjoy and the things you are good at. It might give you inspiration.

Starting your own business at an early age can have drawbacks. Opening a bank account and selling through online websites will mean you will need an adult to help you. Do you know anyone who has started their own business? Is there a teacher at your school who is interested in supporting young entrepreneurs? These people may act as your mentors to help you through the process.

I love making fudge.

I like writing.

BUSINESS IDEA 1

Really healthy snack company snack products

 You think you have identified a gap in the market for a product.

Your school has banned fizzy drinks and sugary snacks. Your classmates are complaining that the healthy snacks and drinks on offer at break time are boring.

 **The business idea**

To create a range of healthy, exciting, tasty snacks that can be sold at break time in your school.

Think carefully about your idea. Can you see any obvious problems?

Problems and solutions

The school may not be happy about you selling food.  Explain your idea to the relevant teachers, asking for their permission. Offer to give part of the profit to a charity or to support a school project.

You do not have a kitchen you can use. Teachers may be willing to let you use a kitchen in school to prepare your snacks.

Pupils do not have much money to spend on snacks. Keep the cost of raw materials and packaging as low as you can.

FINDING THE RIGHT PRODUCT

Sensible entrepreneurs spend time doing research before they start up their business. Look at what snacks are already available at school. Find out what your customers are looking for in a mid-morning snack and what they are willing to spend on it.

The Internet

Research which snack ingredients are healthy.

Books and magazines

Look at adverts for existing healthy snacks to get ideas.

Product research

Supermarkets

Look at the ingredients' panels on the back of healthy snacks. Also make a note of prices.

The competition

Have a look at what is available in the school canteen and make a note of the prices.

Legal requirements

When you start a business you need to check that what you are doing is legal and complies with legislation in the country you are in. Legal requirements vary so ask an adult to help you find out what you need to do BEFORE you start. Guidelines for preparing food are there to make it safe for everyone, so it is important that you follow them properly.

Market research

The place you are going to sell your product is known as the market. This might be your high street, the Internet or your school. Finding out about the market for your product is called market research.

Types of market research

- Surveys
- Interviews
- Questionnaires

You have identified your market as your school. Now do some market research.

Design a questionnaire to find out what people would like in a new, healthy snack product.

Write down a list of ten healthy ingredients. Ask people to rate them from 1–10 in order of preference.

If they already buy a snack at break time, ask them these questions:

- What snacks do they buy?
- How much do they spend on snacks?
- Would they consider buying an alternative?

At school, ask as many people as you can to fill in your questionnaire.

What did you find out?

Most popular snack ingredients

1 Popcorn;
2 Nuts;
3 Coconut;
4 Dried apple;
5 Apricots.

Price

Students are prepared to pay between 50p and 70p for a snack.

Competition

The top competition is a cereal bar that costs 60p.

TRY THINGS OUT

Use your market research to design a snack product to meet the needs of your customers.

Taste testing

Make up small batches of a range of products containing the most popular ingredients.

Popcorn bars
- Popcorn and nut bars
- Popcorn and dried fruit bars
- Popcorn-coconut-apple bars

Popcorn cones
- Paper cones of popcorn, nuts, seeds and dried fruit in different combinations

Cones of popcorn in natural flavours
- Popcorn flavoured with cinnamon, chilli or salt

Offer free tastings at break time. In return ask people to answer some questions about which product they prefer.

- On a scale of one to ten how would you rate each product?

- Are there any reasons why you would not buy any of the products?

If not many people like your product you may have to think of another idea. Better that than spend money setting up a business that is not going to succeed!

Product range

From the result of this feedback you can design your final product range. For example:

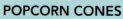

POPCORN CONES
Paper cones filled with popcorn

POPCORN POTS
Two varieties: popcorn and nuts, and popcorn and dried fruit

THE RIGHT PRICE

It is important to work out exactly what profit you will make from the things you sell.

Calculate the cost of each ingredient

1 Find out where you can buy the best popcorn for the cheapest price.

2 Work out exactly how much popcorn is needed for each product.

3 Do this for all the ingredients. Add together the cost of all the ingredients in each snack. This will give you the cost of one item.

4 Divide the price of each bag of popcorn by the amount in each individual product to give you the cost of the popcorn in the snack.

Calculate the cost of packaging

The popcorn pots are going to be sold in tubs made from recycled plastic. The popcorn cones will be handmade from baking paper.

1 See where you can buy baking paper and plastic pots for the cheapest price.

2 Work out how much paper is needed to make one cone.

3 Divide the price of a roll of baking paper by how much you need for each product. This will give you the cost of the packaging.

Add together the cost of making and packaging one item. **This is the unit cost**.

The difference between the unit cost and the selling price is your **profit margin**.

If you sell each pot at a price people at school can afford, can you make a profit? If not, go back and look at the costs again and adjust them until you can.

A HEALTHY IMAGE

Branding is the image that your company and your products have in the market. Over time customers begin to recognise a brand that they like and will buy it in preference to the competition. They will have developed brand loyalty.

Brand image

Decide what brand image you want to put across to your customer.

Fun **Healthy** **Exciting** **Tasty**

USPs

Are there things that make your product better than the competition, such as healthy ingredients and lack of additives or preservatives? These are your Unique Selling Points (USPs).

Business names

A good business name is very important. It can be something memorable or it can describe the business. Do not choose a business name that limits you in the future. *Popcorn Snacks* may sound good, but what if you decide to develop a range of snacks that do not contain popcorn? When you have decided on a name, design a logo to reinforce the message.

The business name could be:

Really healthy snack company

Product name

This is the name that will be on the product label. It needs to be memorable, such as:

Pop Cones or Pop Pots

I love popcorn.

And it is healthy, too.

Labelling

Customers want to know what is in the food they eat. If they have allergies, this information is vital. Write down all the things in your products and design labels so that they can clearly read the ingredients.

Managing waste and recycling

The paper and plastic is recyclable. Next to where you sell the snacks, place a recycling bin for the empty bags or pots.

LIGHT BULB MOMENT!

To reduce waste, you could offer a reduced price refill service for customers who bring back their pot to be filled up.

PLANNING

Do I need a business plan?

The answer is that unless you need money to set up your business (see pages 16–17) you do not, but sensible entrepreneurs want to know that they are putting their efforts into something that has a good chance of being a success.

What is a business plan?

A business plan is everything you know about your business written down in one place. You can show it to people or use it as reference so that you can fully understand what you are doing and why you want to do it. A business plan for a small start-up does not have to be complicated – see the summary opposite.

Pitching your idea

If you are looking for a sponsor or are selling the business idea to a mentor or a teacher at school, you will need to give them a summary of the business. This is known as a pitch. A pitch is a short presentation summarising your business idea and answering questions about it.

This may seems scary but as an entrepreneur you will need to learn to sell ideas, so now is a good time to start.

✓ Do the research. A pitch is easy if you know the facts.

✓ Make notes of the most important things you want to say.

✓ Practise in front of a mirror or practise giving your presentation to a friend.

✓ Keep it short – about two minutes is usually perfect.

✓ Try to look confident.

A BUSINESS PLAN

Summary

The first part of a business plan is a summary. That sounds odd because a summary is usually at the end of something, but it is placed at the front so that the person reading it can understand the business from the beginning. Write it last as by then you will have all the information you need.

The business idea

Are you selling products or services? Describe what you intend to sell or the services you can provide.

Goals

Why do you want a business? Do you want to raise money to buy a new phone or turn your business into a global success?

About you

What have you done that will help you to set up and run a business?

Finance

Information about costing and pricing your products or services. Calculate the money you need to set up the business and run it until you begin to get money back into the business from customers.

The market

Describe the customers who will buy your products or services. Describe the competition you will face.

Market research

What market research have you done? See pages 9 and 10.

Why will you succeed when lots of businesses fail?

In two columns write a list of your:

Strengths	**W**eaknesses
Opportunities	**T**hreats

This is called a **SWOT** analysis.

MONEY, MONEY, MONEY

To start your business and run it until you make money you will need money for stock, packaging, printing and raw materials.

Assets are money or things that you already have that can be sold to raise money.

Money

- Do you have any savings that you could use to start your business?

- Can you earn some money doing odd jobs for family and friends?

- Do you have any old toys, electronic devices or hardly worn clothes that you no longer want? If so, you could sell them – but ask permission first.

Other assets

- You can sell clothes in good condition on the Internet through online auction sites such as ebay and Gumtree.

- If you have a lot of unwanted stuff, you could have a garage sale or ask an adult to help you sell at a car boot sale.

BIG SALE!

Other ways to get funding

Crowdfunding

This is a way of raising small amounts of money from a lot of people to start a business. Use the Internet to research more information.

Gifts

Family and friends may be prepared to give you money to start your business.

Seed funding

Entrepreneurs who do not have any assets have to raise money to start a business. Money raised to start a business that has not yet started to trade is sometimes known as seed funding. Like a seed, it is the first small stage in something that will grow bigger.

Businesses go to banks to fund their projects. The agreement is called a loan and when the business is making money, the loan is paid back. However, banks charge interest to lend money so you will end up paying back the loan plus the interest. Family or friends may give you an interest-free loan which means that you will only pay back what you borrowed.

If family and friends loan you money, you must make it clear to them that there are risks. If the business does not work out, you will not be able to pay them back.

Loan

If you are asking someone for a loan you can give them your business plan to read. This should give them the information they need to make a decision.

If you do not have a business plan, be prepared to answer questions about your business (see page 15).

What is your business idea?

How much money do you need?

What market research have you done?

What product research and testing have you done?

What is the money for?

MAKING THE SNACKS

All the processes that turn raw ingredients into a finished product are called the production.

Production

Think about all the stages in making a POP POT.

Weigh out the popcorn for one pot.

Weigh out the almonds for one pot.

Weigh out the raisins for one pot.

Put the ingredients into a pot.

Put on a lid.

Shake the pot to mix up the ingredients.

Is this the best way to organise the production of your product? Would it save time to make up all the pots of the same flavour in a batch? If you have people to help you, each person could have a different job in the production of the finished pots.

- Are you going to make all the products?

- It is possible that you are better at selling them than making them.

- If you cannot do both, you will have to work out how much you have to pay someone else to make the products for you. Can you still make a profit?

Quality

School kitchen staff are trained to meet health and safety guidelines for the safe preparation of food. Ask for their advice about things such as covering your hair or using disposable gloves.

Consistency

To keep your customers happy you need to make sure that the product they buy is the same every time they buy it. Write down the recipe for each pot so that you can make it the same every time.

Stock

Your stock is the number of products you have made up ready to sell. Should you make up a lot of stock?

✗ No

- Ingredients may go off.

- When you are making food products, the ingredients you use will all have sell-by dates. The snacks in the POP POTS will therefore have a sell-by date no later than those of the ingredients.

- You will need somewhere appropriate to store stock safely.

- You will tie up your money in products that are waiting to be sold.

✓ Yes

- Raw ingredients are cheaper if you buy them in large quantities.

- It is more efficient to make a lot at one time.

**SELL-BY DATE
14.08.2019**

Stock control

Ideally you will have just enough stock to make up orders for the product without running out. To do this you need to keep an eye on your levels of stock as well as the levels of your raw ingredients. This is called stock control.

COOKING BLOGS AND VLOGS

Is there a particular style of cooking that you are passionate about? Why not set up a blog or vlog (video blog) so that other people can share your passion and pick up tips.

Why set up a blog?

A blog is cheaper to set up than a business selling products or services. The disadvantage is that it can take a long time to start earning money from it.

To set up a blog you will need:

✓ A reasonable camera or smartphone.

✓ A blog site. Some blog sites, such as WordPress and Tumblr, can be set up for free. Log in and follow the instructions to create a domain name (see page 31) and design your site. If you want a vlog site then go to YouTube.com and create a channel for your videos.

✓ Somewhere to work where you will not be interrupted.

✓ Cooking equipment. The permission of your parents or an adult to use the space and the equipment.

✓ Ingredients. You can eat the finished product.

To set up a vlog site you will also need:

✓ A reasonable video camera or smartphone and maybe someone to operate it. Your hands will be occupied with cooking!

Be very careful about what you say on social media. Do not do or say anything that you may regret later. Stay safe online by never giving out your address or phone number.

BUSINESS IDEA 2

Veggies vlog

You and a friend have been vegetarian for a long time and love to cook vegetarian food. You also know a lot about the foods you need to eat to maintain good nutrition and health.

The business idea

In partnership, to create a weekly vlog called Veggies. The videos will talk about what you have cooked and eaten that week and they will be linked to a blog site with recipes and advice.

What to do:

Make videos showing how to make your recipes of the week. Keep them short, editing out any boring bits.

Type out the recipes to go along with the videos so that people can print them and keep them.

Take photos of the finished dishes to post on the site.

Upload the videos to your site via YouTube.

Upload the written content and photos to your blog site.

How to make money from the site

- If enough people follow your blog, manufacturers might send you free stuff to review. To increase your followers link to Facebook, Twitter and Instagram. Tweet about your blog. Send photos via Instagram. Sign up to Google Analytics. Update your Facebook page regularly about what you are doing and keep adding content to the site.

- Apply for Google AdSense. If you are accepted, advertisers will bid to put adverts on your site and you will be paid every time someone clicks on one of them. To be accepted you need interesting information on your blog.

BAKING FOR MONEY

Some businesses offer a service that people pay for. Can you cook simple meals or bake great cakes? If the answer is YES then providing a cooking service may be a business that will work for you.

BUSINESS IDEA 3

Sunday treat cake delivery company

> ! You want to set up a baking business but you can only bake at weekends because of homework commitments.

From talking to family and friends you have found that they would like to eat a homemade cake at the weekend but do not have time to make one. They prefer local ingredients with no additives, linked to high animal welfare.

The business idea

To set up a cake making and delivery service. To use free- range eggs and local ingredients wherever possible. To bake and deliver at the weekend.

I love a homemade lemon drizzle cake at the weekend.

Me too and now I don't have to make it.

What to do:

✓ Make a list of the cakes you know you can make well.

✓ Design a leaflet and order form with information about your business. Include a list of the cakes on offer, as well as a list of ingredients and details about local suppliers of ingredients. Give clear information about how people can order and pay for cakes.

✓ Give the leaflet to people you know first. They can be used for market research. If they order, you can follow up the order by asking them what they thought of the product and the service.

✓ Ask people for a 50 per cent deposit with the order to cover the cost of ingredients and cake bags.

✓ Cost out each ingredient (see page 11). Do not forget to include the cost of cake bags. Estimate the cost of delivering the cakes. Work out how much to charge so that you make a profit.

Terms and conditions

These may seem boring but they are there to protect both you and your customer. They do not need to be complicated. Think of the things that may go wrong and write down what you would do. For example, what would you do if you deliver a cake and there is no one at home?

BAKING FOR CHARITY

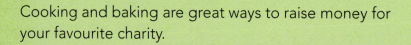

Cooking and baking are great ways to raise money for your favourite charity.

BUSINESS IDEA 4

My favourite recipe cake sale

The business idea

To run a cake sale for a charity. Ask people for permission to use their favourite recipes to bake the cakes and biscuits.

Lots of charities run special baking events. Look on the Internet to see if you can get a fundraising kit with everything you need.

The key to a successful sale is planning.

Things to do well in advance

Choose a location

Find somewhere where lots of people will pass by, such as a high street, a school or a fête.

Choose a day

If you are not part of a national event, make sure the day you choose does not clash with any sporting events or TV shows that might keep people at home.

Book a pitch

Popular locations (or pitches) can be fully booked for weeks ahead.

Visit the pitch

Find out what is included. Do they provide a table, a chair or protection from the weather?

Things to do two weeks before the sale

✓ Find as many people as possible to help you make cakes. If they do not have time to bake a cake, ask people if they could donate ingredients or help sell cakes on the day.

✓ Give your bakers a short list of hygiene instructions about baking for public consumption.

✓ Ask your cake bakers to write a list of the ingredients in each cake. If it is not a secret, they could include the recipe too.

✓ Make a poster explaining that all the money goes to charity.

✓ Decide on prices.

✓ Let people know where to deliver their cakes.

✓ Advertise your cake sale in as many places as possible.

Things to take on the day:

✓ Cash box and a float.

✓ Stick-on price tickets.

✓ Poster (see above) explaining that all the money goes to charity.

✓ Roll of food bags and cake bags to protect the cakes.

✓ Table and tablecloth if needed.

! If you are outside, be prepared for any type of weather. A plastic sheet is a good idea to cover up the baked goods if it rains. A sunshade will help preserve them on a hot day.

HAVE YOU THOUGHT OF THIS?

Once your business is set up, look closely at the information you have to see if you can make more money from it.

Expand your product range

Veggies

Put all your recipes into an online vegetarian cookbook. Add an e-commerce plugin to your website so that customers can pay to download it. Search the Internet for information on how to do this.

Really Healthy Snack Company

Add new products, such as breakfast pots filled with homemade low-sugar muesli, and bottled flavoured water.

Sunday Treat

Offer Sunday afternoon tea as a package – cakes, scones and sandwiches.

Look at the information you already have and see how you can use it in other ways.

The recipes will make a fantastic cookbook.

I will buy some as gifts.

MY FAVOURITE RECIPE
Cake sale

Turn all the favourite recipes into a book and make copies to sell.

PROMOTION

Letting people know that your business and products exist is called promotion.

Here are just a few of the ways you can promote your business:

Advertising

Put an advert on the notice boards in places where potential customers will see it.

Local radio

It costs money to advertise a business on local radio, but if you hold an event or do something newsworthy they may run a feature on you.

Newspapers and magazines

Reporters are always keen to write about interesting local news items. Ring the news desk of your local newspaper and tell them what you are doing.

Facebook

Post regularly on your business Facebook page. Ask questions and read your feedback.

Twitter

Tweet regularly about new products and events. Follow people who are in similar businesses.

Personal recommendation

If you have a good product your customers will tell their friends about it.

NOW WHAT?

✓ You have created a successful business

Whatever your business, one thing is certain – things will change. The market will change, tastes will change and *you* will change.

To stay profitable, all businesses must adapt and be flexible.

Keep in touch with your customers

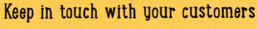

Email, Twitter, market research – use every means you can to get feedback from your customers.

Add new products and services and remove the ones that do not make money.

If you are successful it is likely that someone will start up a similar business. How will you cope with competition?

Brand loyalty

If people have been very happy with your products they may prefer to buy what they already know.

Customer service

If you have been giving a high level of customer service, they may not want to go elsewhere.

Loyalty offer

Offer an incentive for their loyalty, such as a loyalty card.

THEN

It is up to you! It is your business and you can decide. Are you still passionate about your business or do you want to take what you have learned and start again? Many entrepreneurs start more than one successful business.

✗ Your business is not making money

You have tried your best but your business is not making money. What should you do?

Sole trader

Meet any outstanding orders, sell off any stock and stop trading.

Partnerships

Decide between you what to do. Your partner might like to carry on without you. If not, meet any outstanding orders, sell off stock and stop trading.

Try to work out what went wrong

You will have learned a lot by starting up a business. Do you know why your business idea did not work?

Was your product or service too expensive?

Was your product or service too cheap for you to make money?

THEN

Take all the lessons you have learned while setting up the business, go back to page 6 and start all over again! Very few successful entrepreneurs achieve success with the first business they set up. What they have in common is that they refuse to let it put them off trying again.

'FAILURE IS NOT THE OPPOSITE OF SUCCESS. IT IS A STEPPING STONE TO SUCCESS.'

Arianna Huffington (1950–), American author and businesswoman

BUSINESS JARGON

A glossary of business words and expressions

A

advertising Activities, such as displaying posters, placing adverts or broadcasting adverts on TV, that attract attention to products or services.

assets In business, money, property or things of value that are owned by the business.

B

blog A website set up to encourage and interact with its followers, or an article posted on a website.

brainstorming A way of coming up with creative solutions by encouraging people to suggest everything they can think of, however improbable.

brand The type of product produced by a company or the image that a business has created of itself (of quality, low-cost, luxury etc).

business An organisation that makes goods or provides services, and sells them for money.

business plan A report that includes all the research about a business idea, including how it aims to make money.

C

company Any type of business that trades goods or services.

consumer In business, the person who buys a product or service.

customer Someone who buys products or services.

customer service The help and advice given to customers by a business.

D

deposit A sum of money paid in advance of goods or services being received.

domain name A domain name is a unique name used to identify a website.

E

e-commerce (electronic commerce) Buying and selling over the Internet.

entrepreneur Someone who starts a business, taking on the responsibility for the risks and rewards.

expertise Knowledge and experience of a subject.

F

feedback A customer's reactions to a product or service, which can be used to improve the performance of a business.

G

goods A physical product, such as a cake or a car, that can be sold to supply a want or a need.

I

interest In relation to a loan of money, the regular payment of an agreed sum of money until the loan is repaid.

L

legislation Laws passed by a government.

loan Money lent from one person or organisation to another.

logo A recognisable symbol or name for a company.

loyalty In business, when customers buy again.

M

market A place where goods or services are traded for money, such as a shop or a website.

market research Gathering information about the market for a product or service.

marketing All the activities needed to sell a product or service, including advertising, promotion and sales.

mentor A person with experience who acts as an advisor to someone with less experience.

P

packaging The materials used to contain and protect products during shipping.

partnership A business owned by two or more people.

pitch A presentation summarising a business idea. Also, a place to set up a market stall.

post On websites, a blog entry.

product An item that has been manufactured for sale.

production The process of making a product.

profit The amount of money left over once costs have been deducted from sales.

promotion Ways of letting people know that your business and products exist.

Q

questionnaire A list of questions used to collect information about a specific subject, product or service.

R

raw ingredients The uncooked ingredients (eggs, butter, sugar, flour) used to make a cake or a meal.

raw materials The materials used to make a product.

recycle To reuse products or materials.

research To find out more information about something.

risk In business, the possibility of making a loss.

S

seed funding Money raised to start a business. Like a seed, it is the first small stage in something that will hopefully grow into something bigger.

self-employed Someone who runs their own business or works for themselves.

services Activities, such as banking or hairdressing, that can be sold to customers.

social media Websites or apps (applications) that enable people to communicate by creating and sharing content over the Internet.

sole trader One person owning a business.

sponsor Someone who provides funds or support for a project.

start-up A new business set up for the first time.

start-up costs The one-off costs of starting a new business.

stock The goods or products that are ready to sell (stored in a shop or warehouse).

stock control Controlling the level of stock so that customers' orders can be fulfilled.

SWOT analysis An analysis of the Strengths, Weaknesses, Opportunities and Threats of a business.

T

terms and conditions The rules that form part of an agreement between a business and its customers.

U

unit cost The cost of making a single product.

USPs (Unique Selling Points) The things that make a company or a product stand out from its competitors.

V

vlog A video blog.

Further information

www.hoodamath.com/mobile/games/lemonadestand.html
There are various versions of this game on the Internet where the challenge is to run a profitable lemonade stand. You can change the recipe, price and quantity to maximise the profits.

www.youtube.com/user/CharlisCraftyKitchen on YouTube
Watch a successful cookery vlog, such as Charli's Crafty Kitchen, and see if you can pick up some tips.

https://uk.godaddy.com/help/what-is-the-difference-between-a-domain-name-and-a-website-16574
A simple explanation of what a domain name is, why you need one and how to set one up.

http://bizkids.com/business-resources
These business resources should help inspire you.

Note to parents and teachers: every effort has been made by the Publishers to ensure that these websites are suitable for children, that they are of the highest educational value, and that they contain no inappropriate or offensive material. However, because of the nature of the Internet, it is impossible to guarantee that the contents of these sites will not be altered. We strongly advise that Internet access is supervised by a responsible adult.

INDEX

These are the list of contents for each title in the How to make money series.

How to make money from cooking and baking

Why start a business? · Finding a business idea · Finding the right product · Try things out · The right price · A healthy image · Planning · Money, money, money · Making the snacks · Cooking blogs and vlogs · Baking for money · Baking for charity · Have you thought of this? · Promotion

How to make money from your computer

Why start a business? · Selling on the Internet · Create a brand · Blogs and vlogs · Review blogs · Showcase your talent · Crazy stuff · Ways to monetise · Making money from apps or games · Money, money, money · Selling computer services

How to make money from upcycling

Why start a business? · Product design · The market · Marketing · Branding · Selling on the Internet · How to sell at a craft fair · An upcycling blog or vlog · Production · Inventions · People, planet, profit · Running your business · Setting up a website

How to make money from your spare time

Why start a business? · The idea · Research · Target marketing · Creating a brand · Pricing · Production · Selling · The Internet · Use your skills · Offer a service · Get SMART · Work part-time